LOSING
A LOVE,
FINDING
A LIFE

Books by Susan Jeffers

Feel the Fear and Do It Anyway: Dynamic Techniques for Turning Fear, Indecision, and Anger into Power, Action and Love*

Feel the Fear . . . And Beyond: Dynamic Techniques for Doing It Anyway

Dare To Connect: How to create confidence, trust and loving relationships*

Opening Our Hearts to Men: Taking Charge of our Lives and Creating a Love That Works*

End the Struggle and Dance with Life: How to Build Yourself Up When the World Gets You Down*

Losing a Love, Finding a Life: Healing the Pain of a Broken Relationship

Thoughts of Power and Love

The 'Fear-Less' Series:

> *Inner Talk for . . . A Confident Day**
> *A Love That Works**
> *Peace of Mind**

* Also available on audiotape

LOSING A LOVE, FINDING A LIFE

HEALING THE PAIN OF A BROKEN RELATIONSHIP

SUSAN JEFFERS

PIATKUS

© 1992 Susan Jeffers PhD

First published as *The Journey from Lost to Found*
in Great Britain in 1993
by Judy Piatkus (Publishers) Ltd
of 5 Windmill Street, London W1P 1HF

This edition published in 1998

Reprinted 1998

The moral right of the author has been asserted

A catalogue record for this book is
available from the British Library
ISBN 0-7499-1799-1

Designed by Zena Flax

Set in Plantin by
Phoenix Photosetting, Chatham, Kent
Printed and bound in Great Britain by
Mackays of Chatham PLC, Chatham, Kent

TO THE LIGHT

WITHIN US ALL

My life is beautiful,

   I have it all . . .

But even in the sunshine,

   One has to cry sometimes.

CONTENTS

PREFACE   11

IN THE BEGINNING   13

THE END OF AN ERA   17

THE SEARCH   55

MOMENTS ALONG THE WAY   77

COMING HOME   135

EPILOGUE   159

PREFACE

The contents of this book may surprise you. Long before I became an author of self-help books and a teacher in the area of personal growth, I was very fearful and needy of help myself. It was 1972. My first marriage was crumbling and I was feeling very empty and lost.

To help me get through this difficult, sometimes overwhelming, period of my life, I would find solace in sometimes jotting down the feelings I was experiencing, usually on any piece of paper that happened to be handy at the time – an old envelope, a wrinkled sales slip, a gum wrapper, a note pad or whatever. Later, when I would discover one of my scribblings at the bottom of my purse or lying somewhere around the house, I would throw it into a little box sitting on my shelf.

Two years passed. One Sunday afternoon when I had some time on my hands, I opened the little box and began to arrange my many pieces of paper in chronological order. I was astounded at the sequence of discovery that emerged. On these pieces of paper, collected over a two-year period, I was able to trace the Journey of a person who had lost a love, but found a life. I had travelled from a place called Lost to a place called Found. My Journey included blame, despair, hurt, anger, discovery, laughter, joy, bliss and every other human emotion. Little did I know that these thoughts, written over time, would be the seeds of much that I write about and teach today.

Whether you are in a relationship or not, you will see yourself in much of what you are going to read. Many of you have made the same Inner Journey as I have and will identify with my struggle and ultimate sense of triumph.

Many of you are still feeling lost. My experience will give you the faith that, step by step, it is possible for you to pull yourself out of your pain and loneliness . . . and find your way home. Always remember that you are not alone. You are a part of the human family. And each of us, in our own way, has to make this poignant, profound – and sometimes painful – Journey from Lost to Found.

IN THE
BEGINNING

We thought one got married and lived happily
ever after;
   We didn't know that relationships require
   hard work . . .

We thought we couldn't ask for what we needed;
   We didn't know that no one is a mind reader . . .

We thought all of our needs should have been
filled with marriage;
   We didn't know what our most important need
   was – a sense of self . . .

We thought our becoming one made us whole;
   We didn't know two whole people were necessary
   from the start . . .

We thought he had to be strong and take care
of her;
   We didn't know we were supposed to take care
   of each other . . .

We thought it was disloyal to grow as an
individual;
   We didn't know how stifling too much
   togetherness could be . . .

We thought when the other grew, it was a threat;
  We didn't know we were each good
  enough and shouldn't feel threatened . . .

We thought those who asked for help were weak;
  We didn't know everyone needs help . . .

We thought money would make us secure;
  We didn't know that security meant knowing
  you can make it – with or without money . . .

We thought the other wasn't giving;
  We didn't know we weren't receiving . . .

He thought I was happy;
  He didn't know how frightened I was . . .

I thought he was happy;
  I didn't know how frightened he was . . .

We didn't know . . .
  We just didn't know . . .
    There was so much we didn't know . . .

THE END
OF
AN ERA

So many of us live our lives with
a feeling of depression born from our
imagined helplessness. We depend
on others to provide our happiness –
seemingly unable to find it ourselves.

What is it that we *really* want?

Most of us don't even know . . . that we
don't know . . . what we want out of life.

We don't know . . . that we don't know . . .
what makes us happy.

All we know is that our mate isn't funny all the time,

   or clever all the time,

   or considerate all the time,

   or rich all the time,

   or handsome all the time,

   or whatever . . . all the time,

not recognizing that if he were all those things all of the time, *we would still be looking for more.*

Such an impossible burden we place on people we *pretend* to love! Asking them to give us what we want, when we don't even know what we're looking for!

And so, the years pass. The resentment
grows all around and we blame each other,
instead of understanding,
'Hey, I'm asking you the impossible!
I'm asking you to give me myself!'

Slowly and imperceptibly, it becomes
too late. The bitterness and hostility
are too much to live with.
And we wake up one morning and say,
'*My God, what happened?*'

I don't turn you on any more,

That's a real turn off;

You don't let me in any more,

I prefer to stay out.

Your fear creates a need for

separation; mine creates a need for closeness.

Who said opposites attract?

I feel your love . . . and I feel your

total resistance to loving me.

When I feel your hostility, I feel ugly.

It is so difficult for me to reach out to you

then. I withdraw and become hostile

as well. It's such a pity. All that we are

really both asking for is to be loved.

When I feel your hostility, YOU become ugly.

If I could only have compassion for

the wounded child behind your mask. But it's

so hard to have compassion for someone you

want to punch in the face!

You have in your head a picture about what

our life is supposed to be. You expect

that I will fit right into your picture. You

forget that I, too, have a picture about what

our life is supposed to be. And right now,

you don't fit my picture!

I wonder why we always demand that
it be the way 'it's supposed to be'.
Why can't we simply enjoy the way it is?

Don't insist I behave in a certain way

because society says I'm supposed to.

Just look around!

What does society know anyway!

It's time I start doing things
because I choose to do them, not
because I'm supposed to do them.
It's time I start writing my own script!

As my daughter once beseeched me,
'If you can't wear whatever socks you want,
what's left in life?!?'

You started out as my best friend, but

you have become my worst critic. I don't think

that's what friendship is about!

Whoever he wanted all those years is
not the me that is emerging. The more I
become ME the less he likes me . . .
and the more I like myself.

I have to be who *I* want me to be . . .
whatever the price.

He never really loved ME.
He *loved loving* me.
He loved the image of me that
he created as his wife . . . but
he didn't really love ME.

No, he didn't really love ME . . . any more
than I really loved HIM.

A special friend once told me,
'He sets you a banquet table and never
brings you any food.'

He seems empty to me . . .
an empty suit. Is he empty?
Or am I?

It appeared from the outside looking in
that I had it all, yet I was starving.
We both were.
It's hard to give to someone when
you are empty inside.

Before I could change, I had to recognize
that life is too short to walk around feeling . . .

angry all the time,

hurt all the time,

empty all the time,

alone all the time.

The beginning was glorious because
we were playing fairy tale roles. We wanted
it to last forever.

Alas! Things don't last forever.
They must change and grow. Or, they will
stagnate and die.

He was the King in the castle. He must
have felt terribly threatened when I wanted
to share the throne. Once you've ruled
the Kingdom, it's hard to let it go.

Some couples grow together. We only grew apart – so far apart that our arms couldn't reach each other any more.

How difficult it is to accept the end of
an era. But, perhaps what is more difficult
is to *recognize* the end of an era.

I tried so hard to hide from myself the
possibility of separation. That was just too
unacceptable for my mind to accept.

I finally perceived that in order for me
to become the person I wanted to be, I had
to end my fairy tale marriage. It would be,
as I learned, like dying and returning
from the dead.

I remember the despair . . . the insecurity
of feeling I couldn't survive on my own.
Was there anyone else out there for me?
Or was he the only drink of water
in the desert?

We can't split up . . .
   How could I tell my mother!
We can't split up . . .
   It would hurt the children!
We can't split up . . .
   I couldn't survive alone!
We can't split up . . .
   There's not enough money!
We can't split up . . .
   I would never find anyone else!
We can't split up . . .
   It would mean I've failed!
We can't split up . . .
   He's such a good catch!

We must split up . . .
   Or I will die . . . .

It's reassuring how the spirit of survival in all of us makes us subtly prepare for the ending of a relationship.

We look around, we fantasize, we develop a skill, a hobby, new friends. We read books dealing with the subjects of self-esteem, divorce, 'making it', managing money. We become aware of other couples who are divorcing. We find ourselves seeking out models . . . those who've made it to the other shore.

Slowly, but surely, we prepare for the inevitable – the end of an era.

Sometimes doors are closed for us,
giving us no choice but to move forward.
It's nice to think our most difficult times
are blessings in disguise!

While some endings may be
difficult to accept, acceptance
blessedly ends all the confusion –
confusion that results from trying to
fit old patterns and responses into
healthier ones that are just
emerging. We learn we just can't
put the two together any more . . .
no matter how much our fear makes
us try.

Without accepting the end of one era, we can't throw the full strength of our being into another. We ultimately discover that there's nothing as powerful as a made-up mind!

The nature of growth is that it is always pulling us forward . . . despite how much we try to drag our feet!

Looking back, we clung so close –
so desperately close –
for so many years . . .

I wonder what we were looking for . . .

Ourselves, I guess.

THE
SEARCH

I didn't know it was going to hurt
so much. I wanted the marriage to
end, yet I wasn't prepared for all the
pain . . . the emptiness in the pit of
my stomach . . . tearing me apart.
Is there anything left to look
forward to? Nothing matters. I feel
so alone.

Sometimes the darkness overcomes me.

Bewilderment.

Panic.

Exhaustion.

Nausea.

Hunger.

It has to get better!

The unrelenting anger wells up inside and paralyses me. 'How could you' . . . I say to all those significant ones who have caused me pain . . . especially him. I sit there staring into space, my heart pounding. Then the tears come. So much hurt!

When and how will I get rid of all
that pain? I don't know. In the meantime,
I'll just have to let it be.

Life was incomplete with you . . .
Now it is incomplete without you . . .

I feel like someone has thrown me in the water to teach me how to swim. Maybe later I'll be thankful for the opportunity. Now, I simply feel like I'm drowning.

I'm lost! A whole Saturday to do
anything I want! I've searched my
mind a hundred times and I can't
think of anything I want to do!
Once again the terror comes.
There is nothing I can do to
stop it. Everyone is out there with
someone. I know it. I am the only
one who is alone.

Will I always feel I'm on the outside looking in? Like a poor little girl peeringly longingly through the window on a cold snowy night, yearning to be part of the happy family sitting cozily before the fire?

For the first time in so many years, I am without a MAN. I realize now how much of an appendage I was all those years. There was no me without HIM.

Time with my children, my girlfriends, my colleagues – it was all filling time until I could be with HIM. Without HIM, everything was second best. My world did not count. I lived in his. Without HIM I was just drifting, hoping to find someone else's world to belong to.

I hope, I hope, I hope.

I can stop searching soon.

I hope, I hope, I hope

another HE will soon appear

so I can go on with my life.

I never realized how little I did over the years that was really me. I had no real friends, no hobbies, no interests that weren't totally part of being a couple. Is it any wonder I feel lost?

Where do I hide from myself . . .
that I need someone constantly to
sustain me? My first response to
learning that I will be alone for an
evening or a Saturday is
abandonment. The only one who
really abandons me ever, is me! It
seems I have been gone so long.

It is strange how difficult it is to find out something as basic as 'Who Am I!'. 'Listen to the cues', I'm told. But the cues are so faint. The voice inside me has been walled off with so many layers of conditioning. Will I ever be able to hear that little voice inside me that is trying to be heard? I can't believe I have travelled so far away from the core of my very being.

The Journey inward begins. I start
to ask myself such questions as,
'What *feels* good?' It's funny but I
never paid much attention to that
before. Somehow my life had been
all taken care of. I never knew how
high a price one pays for being
taken care of . . .

So many 'firsts' without HIM . . .

Attending	*my first party*	without HIM
Living through	*my first holiday season*	without HIM
Furnishing	*my first apartment*	without HIM
Taking	*my first trip*	without HIM
Developing	*my first hobby*	without HIM
Hosting	*my first dinner party*	without HIM

Each step taken is a step into the unknown. I feel like a child learning to walk. But with each step I feel a little surer of my ability to handle my life.

But when will the fear go away?

Slowly, very slowly, yet with giant steps forward, time begins to have meaning.

And suddenly one day IT appears.
A connection. An exquisite
moment. A moment when
everything seems OK, safe, perfect.
A moment that I'd created for
myself. I hang on to it for dear life –
but, sadly, it vanishes. What is left,
however, is the knowledge that IT
can exist.

I asked myself what it was
that I had connected with.
And then suddenly, I knew –
I HAD CONNECTED WITH MYSELF!!!
for the first time in my life,
I FELT WHOLE!

Those delicious moments of wholeness were
to come and go . . . appearing more often and
staying around for longer periods of time. And
very slowly, but very surely, I stopped defining
myself in terms of a relationship. The voice
inside became clearer and clearer every day,
letting me know . . . I was coming Home.

MOMENTS
ALONG
THE WAY

My heart is pounding right now,
clueing me into the fact that I'm scared.
I ask myself, 'scared of what?'

I saw someone die today.

Am I scared about the fragility of life?
I don't think so.

Am I scared about being alone?
No, that's not it.

Am I scared about not doing all the
things in life that I want to do?
YES! That's it!

I have so much I want to do. I want to . . . I can't . . . my job . . . my responsibilities. But what about me? When? When do I sit on that beach and just write? When? When do I see the sights I want to see? When? When won't I be afraid to take risks?

I'm afraid if I soon don't start doing what I want to do for me, I'll never be ready to die. After all, what is death? The end of life. But what if you've hardly lived?

I want to let go of so many things
that are familiar and bring me
security – and I'm scared. I gave up
a relationship which didn't work
and in many ways I'm still not free.
My fear keeps me a prisoner.

Risks! Risks!
I must learn to take risks!
It's the difference between being
dead and alive.

Wouldn't it be wonderful to face
new experiences with delicious anticipation
instead of feeling that my teeth
are being pulled!

Why is change – any kind of change –
so frightening?

If you change things often, does
the fear go away?

We shout 'FREEDOM' and don't
know what it means. It is a
borrowed word. When we finally
have a chance to taste it, all we can
shout is 'HELP'!

I thought life was supposed to be comfortable. This thought kept me from experiencing and growing. I've recently learned that *life is not comfortable!* It is . . .

>Alive!
>
>Rich!
>
>Scary!
>
>Challenging!
>
>Dynamic!
>
>Changing!
>
>Painful!
>
>Joyful!

But seldom comfortable . . . if you are growing! *dead* is comfortable – about as comfortable as you can get.

I wonder if I can learn to be comfortable being uncomfortable!?!

Sometimes I feel that I am only glancing
at things I should embrace.

I have to remind myself to keep pushing past my fatigue. That's the only way to get where one wants to go. Climbing back into bed with the covers pulled over my head may feel good for the moment. But life is beckoning me to come out and play.

Part of me wants to surrender –
to give up trying to 'become'.
I want someone to become
for me.

It isn't easy, life. Sometimes even
going toward the fun times seems too much
of an effort. I guess 'easy' is for children!
It's time for me to grow up.

I found out recently that I am very shy.
It's strange, I never thought of myself that
way. In my little world, I feel quite secure.
But take me out of my world and I'm afraid
to reach out, to participate.

I never realized it before. I had a marvellous
defence. I made everyone 'out there' boring.
A perfect excuse to withdraw. What I was
really feeling was 'I don't belong. I'm
uncomfortable here. I'm afraid they won't
like me.' I guess it was ME that I *really*
thought was boring!

It's an impossible situation, I guess.
I meet few men who like strong
women and I refuse to be weak. So
what does all that mean? It means I
don't have a man . . . and some
man out there doesn't have me.
What a pity!

You can have anything in life, but you can't have everything! We have to make choices . . . and then love our choices. I guess that's the real meaning of 'having it all'!

I've made a choice . . . a man who loves
who I am. Or no man. I must learn that
sometimes loneliness goes with the latter.
And that's OK.

One choice that I've made is that
I'll never allow myself to be dominated again.
I must learn to take responsibility
for my life and not blame any HIM.

How do I handle my fear of a man dominating me? I dominate him.

How do I do this?

I flirt with other men . . .

I get angry and sarcastic . . .

I talk about him in the most negative terms . . .

I invalidate him . . .

I judge him . . .

I don't let him in . . .

I leave . . .

What makes us so afraid to reach out and say, 'Love me.' It's so much easier to say, 'Get out of my life. I don't need anyone!' And then we wonder why we are lonely.

It's always relationships that touch the land of
tears that lies deep within me. When there is
no relationship, I can live with the dull throb
of insecurity interjected with some magical
moments here and there.

When I am in a relationship, my insecurity
hits me squarely in the face. Perhaps that's
why relationships are so valuable. They lead
the way to the needy child within . . . the child
we have neglected to love. We would be wise
to give it the kindness and caring it deserves.

I feel icy cold sometimes, feeling I
give myself away. I guess that's a sign of
death to the Soul.

I know I don't love me. I don't know how to love me. Maybe just knowing is a good first step.

I don't know how to relate to a man.
I'm so afraid he'll put me down.
So I act superior all the time. I'm the
know-it-all. Does everyone know
how much I have to learn?

Sometimes I feel so inferior,
it's disgusting.
Sometimes I feel so superior,
it's disgusting.

How many times do I have to repeat the same
pattern? I want to tell him what I am really
feeling. I don't have any reason to withhold.
The problem is that I mask what I am really
feeling even to myself. Therefore, I can't tell
him the truth. I don't know the truth about
myself until it's too late – and then I hurt.

Our society is so 'advanced', yet
too many of us are unable
to fill even the most basic
of human needs – the need
to communicate and to touch.

This age of transition makes a very strange breed:

'I want to be free'	'Why aren't you there when I need you?'
'Don't tell me what to do!'	'Why aren't you taking care of me?'
'I believe in equality!'	'What do you mean you want me to pay half the rent?'

That's me talking! It's amazing how much I remind myself of some 15-year-olds I know!

I have made the decision that
I will live my life with dignity and
love and caring and that I am going
to push through all the barriers
that keep me from doing so. Yes,
that's my decision. We all have
that choice.

To how many people do I need to say . . . 'I'm sorry. I didn't support you when you needed me. I needed to support myself instead. I'm still not as strong as I'd like to be. It makes me very sad. I know I'm getting there, but I'm sorry if I hurt you along the way'?

That many, huh?

To the men in my life . . . How do I want to
relate to you? I want . . .

> to make you only one part of my life . . .
> not my whole life,
>
> to give you the space to be where
> you are . . . not where I want you to be,
>
> to stop being defensive . . .
> and really hear what you are saying,
>
> to relate as a peer . . . not to make
> myself either superior or inferior,
>
> to reach out when you criticize . . .
> not withdraw or become hostile,
>
> to express my feelings – now – with
> no game playing,

to more easily recognize my 'tapes'
and relate to you as you . . . not
someone who hurt me in the past,

to be clear about what I want from
you . . . so I can tell you,

to love the wounded child within you
unconditionally . . . and not hurt it
any more than it's already been hurt.

An insight: When I give, I expect something
back. If I expect to get something back, then
I am not giving . . . I am only exchanging.
I must ask myself,

'Do I really know how to give?'

I always thought of myself as a giving
person. I wonder how many other lies I've
told myself.

I realize I'm a person who can't
take. If someone is there for me
emotionally, I don't handle it very
well. I can't reach out when I am in
pain. Maybe I'm frightened of
being weak after working so hard to
become strong. If I let someone in,
will I lose myself again? I'm afraid
to take that chance.

My head still thinks of exquisite
moments only with a man, yet my
most sublime moments have been
without a man – moments I've
created for myself. When will I stop
listening to my mind and pay
attention to my heart?

More alone-time is necessary. Why
do I shy away from being alone?
Habit, I guess. In the past I was so
accustomed to feeling abandoned
when I was alone. It's still
surprising to know that some of my
most pleasurable times are my
alone-times.

No longer am I standing there waiting
for some man to catch up with me. Rather,
I am standing there waiting for ME to
catch up with me!

I know I am growing. I am alone.
There is no one there for me right now.
I saw two people kissing today.
Instead of feeling the old loneliness
I used to feel, I only felt their joy.

Joyful feelings are so new to me. I
spent so much of my life feeling sad
or angry or down or rotten or
cheated. In truth, I had it all, all
along. I just never saw it before.
And I lose sight of it too often now.
Talk about needing glasses!

On my bus ride home tonight, I learned
two things about me . . .

Even if I'm alone, there are a lot
of people in my life who love me . . .
and I love bus rides!

It's very complicated! I recently learned that all failure is, is getting what you don't want. Success is getting what you want. Pictures create the failure – expectations gone awry.

If you support whatever happens – you can't fail. Supporting it means acknowledging that's the way it is . . . and it's OK with you. What is, is.

When you don't support the way it is, you fail. After all, what is failure? A picture not filled.

Whew! It makes so much sense! Why is it so difficult to understand?

It's amusing that things never turn out the way we plan. When am I going to learn that the picture I create in my head has absolutely no influence on if or when it comes? When am I going to stop trying to control the future . . . and simply let things happen? Wouldn't that be a relief!

I have to learn how to let go.
What I try to control ends up
controlling me.
I tell myself, 'Let go. Let go. Let go.'
Sometimes it's hard.

Sometimes I feel I could conquer the world.
Sometimes I feel so tired. I fantasize at those
'tired' times that I will just sit down in the
middle of the street and someone will come
and pick me up and take care of me. I don't
feel that so much any more, though. The
world seems more and more manageable as I
feel better and better about myself.

A beautiful woman taught me, 'Say YES to your Universe. Whatever happens, say yes to your Universe.' Those words meant little until I allowed their meaning to penetrate my experience. 'Whatever happens, happens. Go with it and learn.' When I am willing to go with my experiences – good or bad – instead of fighting them, it is such a relief! My life just seems to flow!

For a few days now, I have been really wanting to take care of myself. I feel an openness to letting things in. It's a new feeling . . . the realization that I can do whatever I want to do . . . experience whatever I want to experience.

A trip just opened up for me. Great! I want to go! Done!! I don't have to get 'permission' from anyone. I won't pine for anyone when I'm away. I won't feel guilty.

I know there are advantages to a relationship, but I'm beginning to realize that there are also incredible advantages to being unattached! That is . . . once you've connected with yourself.

It was not long ago that I felt controlled.
I felt my freedom was being taken away.

First came the REVELATION:
I allowed my freedom to be taken away!

Then came the REVOLUTION:
'No! I won't do what you demand of me.'

The thrill of entitlement! The freedom
of entitlement! Whatever the cost!

And how does it feel to be free . . .
  to wear the clothes I've always
  wanted to wear . . .
  to say the things I've always
  wanted to say . . .
  to dance the way I've always wanted
  to dance . . .
  to do what I've always wanted to do . . .
  to be what I've always wanted to be . . .

Well, I'll tell you . . .

Whenever I feel that freedom, I become exhilarated!!! I have unbounded energy. I could dance all night and all day. My creativity is unleashed. I want to cry at the pleasure I find within myself.

Very often when I feel free, I feel afraid – but less and less as time goes by. And I know for the first time in my life . . . *I have a chance!*

The lesson of being free is so simple
that it eludes us. We think of
freedom as the unencumbered life,
but it is really the unencumbered
self. To be free is simply to act on
one's truth . . . and to allow no one
else to obscure that truth.

I can't blame him. The lack of
freedom I felt was of my own
creation. In my effort to gain
approval from him, I was denying
myself. It was my choice. I realize I
cannot blame him or anyone else
for my choices in life.

I giggled as I walked down the street the other day as I realized there is nothing anyone can threaten to take away from me. I am alone now and I am whole.

When I stop demanding of myself
and simply ask 'what do I want?' I
have made great strides towards
self-fulfilment.

As I live each day getting more and
more out of life . . . in terms of
what I want out of life . . . my old
fear of death and ageing diminishes
greatly.

The search to reveal the hidden layers of me goes on and on. I used to ask myself when will it end! I now realize it never ends.

We keep unpeeling the layers until the day we die. It's a relief to know I'm not a failure because I haven't hit the core. Yet I wonder when I die, what part of me I will never have known . . .

I used to look to other worlds
thinking 'I wonder what it's like
over there.' I always seemed to be
searching for something. I realize
I'm no longer searching. It's all
here. It's all about seeing the
richness in each new experience.
Good or bad, it's nice to have
tasted it.

The Journey:

from confusion ⟶

to anger ⟶

to hurt ⟶

to pain ⟶

to power ⟶

to love.

Wouldn't it be wonderful if we could skip a few steps along the way?!?

There is such bittersweet pain in the joy that comes from finally beginning to understand the secret of life . . . and I am finally beginning to understand.

And what is the big secret of life . . . the secret I've been avoiding? I AM TOTALLY RESPONSIBLE FOR MY HAPPINESS! It's so frightening . . . yet filled with opportunity! No one to blame, no one to make wrong and ultimately no one to turn to . . . except myself.

COMING
HOME

How did it happen? How did the feeling of contentment that eluded me for so long come to be? I don't know. I just 'lived into it' somehow.

I was constantly told 'find yourself, find yourself!' How do you find yourself? It's funny. I finally found myself and I don't know how I did it. I don't even know what was 'found'! All I know is that I now feel content. I feel good with me.

I love other people and I need them. But I also need whole weekends of being totally alone – an impossibility just months ago. And when I need company, it doesn't have to be a HIM. It can be my female friends, my children, my mother.

I feel whole being with anyone, not 'out in the cold without HIM' as I felt before. I'm no longer on the outside looking in. I'm at the centre of my own Universe. It's such a warm and wonderful world that way. I'm never excluded. It's always *my* party.

I feel so good! I don't know why exactly.
Nothing in my life is resolved – no
permanence – which such a few years ago was
my imagined harbour of safety.

In a few days that one permanent fantasy –
my marriage – will be over legally. But the
peace in that! I have done so much for myself.
Perhaps that's the joy I feel.

I recall the feelings of helplessness,
hopelessness, just like it was yesterday – yet it
really was a lifetime ago.

To find one's own energy – own
purpose – takes time. At first it is
very dark. The loneliness is
frightening. However, once we push
through it, we find a tremendous
reservoir of power. Without
knowing this power is within us,
how can we love anyone else? Fear
is a great barrier to love!

At first, it is difficult to break old habits – it takes time. I guess the toughest habit to break is dependence. We expect someone to carry our burden and we call it love.

There is so much to learn about
who I am. Each day brings new
opportunities and new insights.
Each entry into my book of life,
each new experience – whether
good or bad – I now see as an
opportunity to 'play', an
opportunity to be aware of how I
handle my feelings. I have learned
not to judge myself, just to
recognize and be aware. I know this
acceptance of who I am will allow
what I can become.

The bittersweet memories of it all. A wise man told me a long time ago . . .

We are all travellers. Nothing is permanent. We are like fruit trees. The beautiful petals blow away and sweet fruit emerges. We cannot mourn the fact that the petals have blown away. We must rejoice at the sweet fruit we have become. We must understand that had the petals not blown away, we would not be what we are today. There is unhealthiness in attaching ourselves to things in a world where change is growth. We learn through the scars and hurt, what is right and wrong for us. We must act as a filter, letting in the good and discarding the bad. We can't live with the anger and the hurt. We have to let go – forgive and forget. Remember that you are who you are today because of those past experiences. Let it go. Let it all go. When you can let go, you are left with tranquillity.

When I finally let go, I understood for the first time what he was talking about.

I feel like I'm getting younger. Everything I am learning is making me feel lighter, more childlike. I have stopped taking myself so seriously – even in my intensely serious moments. I guess part of me loves the drama of those gallantly played scenes. I find myself applauding constantly – and laughing hysterically.

What a beautiful Sunday . . . Me alone with Me.
I never knew how content I could be.

It is morning. Arising late. A hot cup of coffee
(there's nothing like that first cup of coffee). *The
Sunday Times*. The music of my apartment or
the quiet of my apartment . . . *as I choose*. I
write, I dance. Even doing my laundry seems
special today. Even paying my bills are a
reminder that I can take care of myself and live
my life . . . *as I choose*.

It is late afternoon. Some peanuts and a cup of
tea as I watch the lightning's magnificence and
hear the mighty claps of thunder. I delve into
my delicious book and a cozy nap overtakes me.

A beautiful night is yet to come. It's a pity that
tomorrow it has to end. The way I feel right now
I could stay alone with me forever.

My life is so rich right now. I know why. Everything I do, I choose to do. I'm no longer filling time. It took me so long to be able to choose anything. I remember those early days of being alone. I couldn't fill an hour. Now, not only can I fill an hour, I can fill a lifetime.

I tried a singles party tonight. I figured, 'What the heck! I'm always complaining that *they* are all married!'

It was a festive party with throngs of people in a beautiful setting. After a while I didn't want to be there – so I left and went to my neighbourhood café to hear my favourite piano player, totally content to be alone enjoying the music.

I asked myself why I didn't want to be at the party. Everyone seemed to be having such a good time. What was the difference between them and me? Then it came to me. They all were there wanting to meet someone – and I didn't. I realized I'm not ready just yet. I like the deliciousness of being unattached. Dates are even an intrusion lately. There are so many things I want to do for me.

No, I'm not ready to meet someone just yet.

I love feeling whole. I wish I had learned the lesson sooner . . . or perhaps it was *too* soon then and the message would have fallen on deaf ears.

I've learned to like who I am. If I
had a friend like me, I would say,
'Now that is an OK person.'
There are many people out there
who would agree. As far as the
others go, I'll just say hello – and
quickly say goodbye.

I know this is just the beginning. Nothing can stop me now. I have reached the top of the mountain and I feel as though I can soar. I worked so hard and fought so many battles in making that Journey inward. But, I would have rather died than not made that difficult Journey. It is the only way I know of to find one's Self.

The joy of becoming whole is always accompanied by tears. Every step towards a healthy body, mind and soul asks that we say goodbye to something familiar. I have never been very good with goodbyes. So, as I sit here feeling healthier than I ever felt before, I am also crying.

We think of our lives in terms of permanence, not moments, and we hang on for dear life. If you think about it, isn't all of life about beginnings and endings. The secret is knowing when to let go. When we try to hang on or re-create instead of going on to a next moment, we can only have lesser experiences. We have to close the past to fully enjoy today.

Only for the moment . . . then we must say goodbye.

If we don't make the Journey inward,
we will forever be alone. Once we find
our Self, we are never alone.

I now know what my next step
must be. I've become strong. I've
learned how to take care of myself.
Now the really difficult part – *to
open my Heart*. I know it has risks.
When the heart opens it is so
vulnerable. It can get wounded so
easily. But I now know I will always
recover. I will always reach the
other shore.

When the Heart opens up, warm tears of both joy and sadness flow easily. Joy . . . from the feeling of oneness with all things that are human. Sadness . . . that we reject so much of what is human.

The sweet tears of softness and appreciation that are now starting to flow reassure me that one day I'll be able to let someone in. Strength tempered with softness is magnificent. I feel very good with my strength. I know I will feel magnificent when I allow the nourishing tears of love in again.

My life is beautiful,

I have it all . . .

But even in the sunshine . . .

One has to cry sometimes.

EPILOGUE

Susan Jeffers finally did allow her Heart to open. And in walked a beautiful Soul named Mark Shelmerdine. Today they are married and together they are discovering what it feels like to truly love and be loved. They practise all the time. And I have it on the best authority that Susan is happier now than she has ever been in her entire life.